6516

SS-Artillerie-Regiment 4

SS-Polizei-Division

A study of German Artillery

Text: Gordon Rottman
Color Plates: Stephen Andrew

Technical Editor: Frank De Sisto
German spell check: Ralph Zwilling

603-609 Castle Peak Road
Kong Nam Industrial Building
10/F, B1, Tsuen Wan
New Territories, Hong Kong
www.concord-publications.com

We welcome authors who can help expand our range of books. If you would like to submit material, please feel free to contact us.

We are always on the look-out for new, unpublished photos for this series. If you have photos or slides or information you feel may be useful to future volumes, please send them to us for possible future publication. Full photo credits will be given upon publication.

ISBN 962-361-107-2
printed in Hong Kong

INTRODUCTION

While this book focuses on SS-Artillerie-Regiment 4 of the SS-Polizei-Division, it is also a general study of German divisional field artillery employed by both the Waffen-SS (Armed Protection Service) and the Heer (Army). This book also studies the same division's SS-FlaK-Abteilung 4 and its anti-aircraft weaponry.

Divisional History

The order-of-battle of the Waffen-SS contained a number of what might be considered "atypical" divisions. Many Waffen-SS divisions came from unusual origins being comprised of subordinate units consolidated from different sources or troops from a variety of national or ethnic groups. The SS-Polizei-Division fell into both categories. For a time it was the only division that could be considered both Heer and Waffen-SS as it contained personnel from both organizations as well as the Ordnungspolizei (Order Police), which was, by far, the most prominent source of the division's personnel. Reichsführer-SS Heinrich Himmler accepted that for the most part they were neither National Socialists nor fully-fledged SS men. For instance, the division's troops were not required to meet SS racial standards. They came from across Germany as well as from Austria, the Sudetenland, former parts of western Poland, and other areas harboring Volksdeutsche (ethnic German peoples).

On 18 September 1939, Adolf Hitler directed that a Heer infantry division be raised from the Ordnungspolizei, augmented by Heer units. As the Ordnungspolizei were a component of the SS, it was realized from the beginning that the new division would be an unusual mix. The Ordnungspolizei were not a viable source of enlisted manpower for the division. All personnel were either officers or NCO equivalents, so the rank-and-file would have to come from other sources. The Heer contributed several hundred trained specialists and technicians, as well as three complete units requiring a high degree of technical training: Artillerie-Regiment 228, Nachrichten-Abteilung 228 (Signals Battalion), and Divisions Nachschubführer 228 (Divisional Supply Leader—Dinafü), the logistical and service organization. The artillery and signals units would not arrive until August 1940 while the division was in France. This was a result of the artillery upgrade ordered by Hitler for Waffen-SS divisions deficient in this area.

The rank-and-file were assigned from the Ordnungspolizei Reserve, a category of young recruits without police or military training, other than what they may have received previously in the Hitler-Jugend (Hitler Youth) and the Reichsarbeitsdienst (National Labor Service). All Ordnungspolizei personnel assigned to the division were rated as detached from that organization for duty with the Wehrmacht (Defense Force), even after the division was formally designated as an SS formation. These men viewed themselves as soldiers detached from the police while still retaining their rights and privileges as police. They did not consider themselves to be SS men. The benefit the Ordungpolizei gained from this arrangement was that it provided un-trained young men to the Heer where they received complete military training and discipline; those released from active service after light wounds were now available for police or administrative duties.

The Ordnungspolizei officers assigned to the division were required to have had World War I military service or to have served in the Heer as a Reserve officer after 1935. This provided some degree of military expertise, which along with their police experience, qualified them to lead combat troops in the field. The lieutnants—platoon leaders—came from two sources: the SS-Junker-Schule (SS-Officer's Cadet School) at Bad Tölz, or the Reserve Heer officer's course. They then transferred to the Schutzpolizei (Protection Police) and received police training at the Polizei-Offiziersschulen at Fürstenfeldbruck or Köpenick. While the division was under the control of the Reichsführer-SS and Chef der Deutschen Polizei, it was administered and trained by the Heer, which also had operational control over it.

Originally the division was going to be designated 300.Infanterie-Division in the Heer sequence, but when activated on 1 October 1939, it was designated simply the Polizei-Division. The organic units designated "228" were re-designated "300," but this designation was short-lived as the number was dropped and "Polizei-" added as a prefix. At that time the Polizei-Division was comprised of:

Stab der Division
Polizei-Schützen-Regiment 1
Polizei-Schützen-Regiment 2
Polizei-Schützen-Regiment 3
Artillerie-Regiment 300 (not yet assigned)
Polizei-Panzerabwehr-Abteilung
Polizei-Pionier-Bataillon
Divisions-Nachrichten-Abteilung 300 (not yet assigned)
Polizei-Sanitäts-Abteilung
Divisions-Nachschubführer 300
Polizei-Radfahr-Schwadron (later Abteilung)
Polizei-Veterinär-Kompanie
Polizei-Feldgendarmerie-Trupp
Polizei-Ersatz-Abteilung I, II, III (rear replacement units)

The division began assembling at Truppenübungsplatz (Troop Training Area) Wandern, near Zielenzig, in October, but was given an unreasonably short time to organize and train. It was by no means a first-line division and was initially issued older or substitute equipment, including many Czechoslovak weapons, as was common for many Waffen-SS divisions. The Czechoslovak weapons were not necessarily a liability though, as they were excellent designs produced by that country's progressive pre-occupation-era arms industry. There were shortages in some categories of weapons, especially crew-served infantry weapons. The artillery and most of the transport columns were horse-drawn with only a limited number of motor vehicles available.

Training was completed at the end of January 1940 whereupon the division was deployed to the Rhine River facing France to perform a "Watch on the Rhine", long considered almost a sacred duty of the German soldier. The division saw little activity during the "Sitzkrieg" (Sitting War), known to the Allies as the Phony War. In April the division was moved north to Waldkirch and began manning the Westwall defenses (what the Allies mislabeled as the "Siegfried Line") along the Upper Rhine. During the early stages of the French Campaign, the division remained in reserve and continued training. In late May the division moved to Neuenburg and prepared to participate in the second phase of the French Campaign, where they were initially held in reserve. Part of the division was then attached to 10.Infanterie-Division, seeing their first action on 9 June 1940 crossing the Ardennes Canal and Aisne River. Elements of the Polizei-Division next fought against a French rear guard unit in the Argonne before again being placed in reserve. The ceasefire went into effect on 24 June; the division had suffered only light casualties.

The division then served as an occupation force in the Paris area for a year; a practical assignment for a formation comprised largely of former and future policemen. During this period the division received 10,000 officer and enlisted replacements of a younger age. This improved the division's combat capabilities somewhat, but some of the older and now "Fronterlebnis" (frontline combat-experienced) men were returned to police and training duties in Germany, thereby partially negating the effect. The number "300" was dropped from the designations of the Artillerie-Regiment, Nachrichten-Abteilung, and Divisions-Nachschubführer and they were prefixed by "Polizei-". The Polizei-Flak-Abteilung was also added at this time. At the end of June 1941 the division was sent by rail to East Prussia.

Operation Barbarossa, the invasion of the USSR, commenced on 22 June 1941 with the Polizei-Division being assigned to Armeegruppe Nord, again, initially, as a reserve. Within a couple of weeks the division was committed to action near Luga. Its first attempt to take the heavily defended bridgehead failed, but a week later it carried the position in conjunction with other divisions. It had been a difficult fight in the forests and swamps where losses were high. October saw the division participating in the envelopment of Leningrad as well as the subsequent brutal siege, where it remained for the rest of the year.

In January 1942 the division moved south to the Wolchow River area, a vast region of swamps and forests defended by the Soviet 2nd Assault Army. This developed into a battle of reducing enemy pockets of resistance with the last being crushed in June. In the interim, on 10 February 1942 the Polizei-Division and its replacement units were formally assigned to the Waffen-SS; its units had the "SS-" prefix added to their designations. The division itself was re-designated SS-Polizei-Division. The Schützen (rifle) regiments were re-designated SS-Polizei-Infanterie-Regimenter 1, 2, and 3 at the same time. On 1 February 1943 they were again re-designated as SS-Polizei-Grenadier-Regimenter 1, 2, and 3. Hitler had directed that Infanterie units of the Heer and Waffen-SS be re-designated Grenadier in an effort to improve the exhausted infantry's morale. In the old Imperial Army, Grenadier units were considered elite infantry.

In January 1943 the division was moved south to the Lake Ladoga area where serious Soviet counterattacks forced the German units in the sector to withdraw. The severe fighting went on into March until the front was more-or-less stabilized. Parts of the division were withdrawn from the line in October and sent to training areas in Bohemia, Moravia and Silesia. There it was rebuilt with new replacements, reequipped, and reorganized as a Panzergrenadier division. For all practical purposes this was a new division and it was assigned a new Feldpost number. A small part of the division remained at the front as a regimental-sized battle group, designated "Kampfgruppe SS-Polizei-Division". This force fought on in the Northern Front until it was disbanded on 21 May 1944. During this period divisional records note that the Polizei-Artillerie-Regiment was frequently cited for its excellent and responsive fire support.

In the meantime the bulk of the division was reorganized as SS-Polizei-Panzergrenadier-Division on 1 June 1943 with the designations for sub-units changed and additional units organized. This occurred at Truppenübungsplatz Heidelager. "Polizei-" was dropped for the designations of the subordinate units, except the Veterinär-Kompanie. While a Panzergrenadier division in name, it still had significant horse-drawn elements rather than being fully equipped with trucks and halftracks. On 22 October the division received a "4." to prefix its designation. It was now organized as follows:

4.SS-Polizei-Panzergrenadier-Division
Stab der Division
SS-Panzergrenadier-Regiment 7 (three battalions)*
SS-Panzergrenadier-Regiment 8 (three battalions)*
SS-Artillerie-Regiment 4 (three battalions)
SS-Flak-Abteilung 4 (two batteries)
SS-Sturmgeschütz-Abteilung 4 (three batteries)†
SS-Panzerjäger-Abteilung 4 (three companies)
SS-Panzer-Aufklärungs-Abteilung 4 (six companies)
SS-Pionier-Bataillon 4 (three companies)
SS-Nachrichten-Abteilung 4 (two companies)
SS-Panzer-Instandsetzungs-Abteilung 4
SS-Kraftfahr-Abteilung 4
SS-Wirtschafts-Abteilung 4
SS-Sanitäts-Abteilung 4
SS-Feldersatz-Abteilung 4 (five companies)
SS-Divisions- Nachschubführer 4
SS-Polizei-Veterinär-Kompanie 4
SS-Feldgendarmerie-Trupp
SS-Kriegsberichter-Zug 4
SS-Panzergrenadier Ausbildungs-und Ersatz-Abteilung 4‡

* These regiments were initially designated SS-Panzergrenadier-Regimenter 1 and 2 from 6 June 1943 and re-designated on 22 October.
† Redesignated SS-Panzer-Abteilung 4 in July 1944, but was still organized and equipped as an assault gun battalion. It now had four companies.
‡ This was a training and replacement unit that remained in the rear and did not accompany the division in the field.

When training and reorganization was completed, part of the division was deployed to northern Greece to conduct anti-partisan operations. There a reprisal was inflicted on the Greeks after partisans ambushed a convoy. In late 1944 the division was sent to the Belgrade, Bulgaria area on the Southern Front, which was being battered by a Soviet offensive. The division saw heavy fighting in January 1945 and was forced to retreat to Slovakia, but was soon withdrawn and sent to northern Germany in the Stettin area. Here the division met yet another Soviet offensive, then moved to Danzig where it was trapped in a major encirclement. After seeing very heavy fighting in April, it was shipped from the Hela Peninsula to Swinemünde. It then fought its way westward across northern Germany to reach the Elbe River where it surrendered to American troops on 2 May 1945. Some elements, apparently separated and left behind, surrendered to the Soviets.

Divisional Artillery: Equipment and Organization

The typical German horse-drawn divisional artillery regiment is examined here. The SS-Polizei-Artillerie-Regiment was similar, but some standard artillery pieces may have been substituted by other ordnance, especially Czechoslovak pieces in the beginning. The regiment was authorized some 2,500 troops and 2,274 horses. The latter drew over 220 wagons and artillery caissons. All of the artillery was horse-drawn. The division was also supposed to be assigned 105 trucks and 40 motorcycles. The former were mainly for hauling ammunition, signals equipment, and other services. The SS-Polizei-Division was allotted fewer motorized vehicles than normal.

Standard artillery organization called for 36 10.5cm le.FH18 or 18(M) leichte Feld Haubitze (light field howitzers), four 10cm (actually 10.5cm) s.K18 schwere Kanone (heavy guns), and eight 15cm s.FH18 schwere Feld Haubitze (heavy field howitzer). The "18" in these weapons' designations referred to a series designation rather than the year adopted (the more usual meaning). Their development began in the late 1920s with production commencing in the mid-1930s. Firing batteries, regimental and battalion headquarters were provided with a total of approximately 30 7.92mm MG34 light machine-guns for self-defense, while most personnel were armed with Mauser 7.92mm Kar98k carbines. Officers and some specialists were armed with Walter 9mm P38 pistols. Foreign-designed carbines and pistols may have been substituted for these individual weapons as well as for the machine guns.

An explanation of the categories of German artillery is necessary here. Light (leichte) artillery included 7.5cm guns and 10.5cm howitzers. Heavy (schwere) included 15cm howitzers, 10cm guns and heavier weapons. The 15cm guns and heavier ordnance such as the 17cm and 21cm pieces, etc. belonged to non-divisional (corps and/or army) artillery units. In the US army the 15cm howitzer would be designated "medium" artillery, but the Germans did not use this category, only light and heavy.

The Haubitze (howitzer) was a relatively short-barreled piece capable of firing a high-trajectory projectile, allowing it to hit targets behind hills and ridges as well as drop rounds atop the target to, for example, penetrate a bunker's overhead cover. The Kanone (cannon), which in the US Army is called a "gun," is a long-barreled weapon capable of longer range (with a flatter trajectory) than a howitzer. The Mörser (mortar) is a large-caliber, short-barreled weapon, which previously might have been called siege artillery. It is comparatively short-ranged and intended for attacking hardened targets or large area targets. The term "Mörser", in German military parlance, referred to a heavy artillery piece; an infantry mortar was called a "Granatwerfer" (grenade projector). The Germans referred to artillery pieces in general, whether a Haubitze, Kanone or Mörser, as a "gun" (Geschütze).

The three general types of divisional artillery had specific roles. The 10.5cm howitzer was a general artillery piece used to attack all sorts of targets. Its main targets were the enemy's frontline positions or attacking forces. The 15cm howitzer was intended to attack targets deeper in the enemy's rear to include command posts, reserve units, assembly areas, and logistics facilities. The 10cm gun was the most specialized piece. This long-range weapon was intended to attack enemy artillery with counter-battery fire. It could also attack other critical deep targets. Many divisions lacked the 10cm battery because of shortages of this weapon. The two most common complaints regarding German artillery was that the various pieces were usually outranged by comparable US and Soviet types and that their overall weight was excessive. A third complaint, attributed to German soldiers, was that there was simply never enough of it! In essence, the Germans were nearly always outgunned by the Allies.

A variety of ammunition was available for German ordnance. The 10.5cm howitzer had the widest selection including high explosive, high explosive sabot (long-range), antitank hollow-change, antitank sabot (high-velocity), incendiary, smoke, illumination (flare), and propaganda (leaflet dispersal). The 10cm gun and 15cm howitzer were provided with high explosive, armor-piercing, and armor-piercing capped projectiles. Armor-piercing capped rounds allowed the projectile to better penetrate the target if striking at a steep angle.

The divisional artillery regiment was organized into four battalions, each referred to as an "Abteilung". This term was used to designate battalion-size units of artillery, armor, reconnaissance, anti-armor, cavalry, signals, and smoke troops. An Abteilung was battalion-sized and organized internally as a battalion with companies or batteries, depending on branch. "Abteilung" is often incorrectly translated as detachment, unit, or division; its literal meaning is "sub-unit". Infantry, pioneers, and some other organizations used the term "Bataillon" in their designations. German Abteilungen were designated with Roman numbers, I. to IV., with IV. (in the case of an artillery unit) being the heavy battalion equipped with 15cm howitzers and 10cm guns. Normally, 12.Batterie was armed with 10cm guns, but the Polizei-Division's IV.Abteilung initially lacked these, being equipped solely with 15cm howitzers.

Each of the Abteilungen were comprised of three firing batteries (Batterie) with each battery containing four howitzers or guns. The batteries were designated by Arabic numbers in sequence throughout the regiment, 1. through 12.Batterie. Since the batteries were so numbered they were normally identified without the inclusion of the Abteilung designation. Therefore, 3.Batterie, I.Abteilung, SS-Polizei-Artillerie-Regiment would be shown abbreviated as "3/SS-Pol-AR". The regiment was organized as follows:

SS-Polizei-Artillerie-Regiment

Regimentsstab mit Stabsbatterie (regimental headquarters and headquarters battery)

I.Abteilung (leichte)
Abteilungs Stabsbatterie (battalion headquarters battery)
1.-3.Batterie (10.5cm le.FH) (firing batteries)

II.Abteilung (leichte)
Abteilungs Stabsbatterie (battalion headquarters battery)
4.-6.Batterie (10.5cm le.FH) (firing batteries)

III.Abteilung (leichte)
Abteilungs Stabsbatterie (battalion headquarters battery)
7.-9.Batterie (10.5cm le.FH) (firing batteries)

IV.Abteilung (schwere)
Abteilungs Stabsbatterie (battalion headquarters battery)
10.-12.Batterie (15cm s.FH) (firing batteries)

Typically a light battalion supported an infantry regiment with the heavy battalion in general support of the division. However, battalions dedicated to support a specific regiment could be redirected to fire in support of an adjacent regiment when necessary. Some or all light battalions could be kept under the artillery regiment's direct control or two or more battalions could be placed in direct support of the division's main assault infantry regiment. This flexibility in the employment of artillery was essential for its successful use. There were times when the Polizei-Division was in reserve, but all or part of the artillery regiment would be attached to other frontline commands for support. When reorganized as a Panzergrenadier division the artillery regiment lost a light battalion. This was because Panzergrenadier divisions had only two Panzergrenadier regiments rather than three seen in infantry divisions.

The initial source of the regiment's units was as varied as that of the troops comprising the division. The units were drawn from existing artillery regiments and consolidated into Artillerie-Regiment 288 on 1 September 1940. The regiment's home station was in Wehrkreis I (Defense District I). The subunits withdrawn from the parent regiments were later reformed from recruits and cadres.

Artillerie-Regiment 288	**Source**
Regimentsstab mit Stabsbatterie	Regimentsstab, AR 85, 101.Inf-Div.
I.Abteilung (leichte)	
Abteilungs Stabsbatterie	Stab, I.Abteilung, AR 107
1.-3.Batterie	3., 6., 9.Batterie, AR 230, 169.Inf-Div.
II.Abteilung (leichte)	
Abteilungs Stabsbatterie	Stab, II.Abteilung, AR 85, 101.Inf-Div.
4.-6.Batterie	3., 6., 9.Batterie, AR 235, 198.Inf-Div.
III.Abteilung (leichte)	III.Abteilung, AR 218
Abteilungs Stabsbatterie	
7.-9.Batterie	
IV.Abteilung (schwere)	IV.Abteilung, AR 235, 198.Inf-Div.
Abteilungs Stabsbatterie	
10.-12.Batterie	

When re-established as a Panzergrenadier division, the artillery regiment was extensively reorganized, now with only three battalions. It's III.Abteilung, now the heavy battalion, received a 10cm gun battery and a regimental observation (Beobachtungs) battery was assigned. The new regiment was activated in October 1943. The guns were towed by either halftrack or truck prime movers. The standard Artillerie-Regiment (motorisiert) was organized as follows:

SS-Polizei-Artillerie-Regiment 4
Regimentsstab mit Strabsbatterie
I.Abteilung (leichte)
Abteilungs Stabsbatterie
1.-3.Batterie (10.5cm le.FH)

II.Abteilung (leichte)
Abteilungs Stabsbatterie
4.-6.Batterie (10.5cm le.FH)

III.Abteilung (schwere)
Abteilungs Stabsbatterie
7.-8.Batterie (15cm s.FH)
9.Batterie (10cm s.K)
Beobachtungs-Batterie

Within the Heer, anti-aircraft units were part of the Artillery branch. Most German anti-aircraft units were assigned to the Luftwaffe for national air-defense, although significant Luftwaffe anti-aircraft units accompanied and supported the Heer Field Army formations. The Heer possessed its own anti-aircraft units assigned to army troops. These units could be attached to corps or divisions as necessary. It was seldom that infantry divisions possessed organic anti-aircraft battalions. When it was reorganized as 4.SS-Polizei-Panzergrenadier-Division in 1943, the division was assigned the new SS-FlaK-Abteilung 4. The Abteilung initially had only one heavy and one light battery, but later received an additional one of each. "FlaK" is the acronym for FliegerabwehrKanone, literally meaning "flyer defense cannon", or, air-defense gun. This battalion was organized as follows:

SS-FlaK-Abteilung 4
Abteilung Stab mit Stabsbatterie
1. und 2.Batterie (schwere) (8.8cm FlaK)
3. und 4.Batterie (leichte) (2cm/3.7cm FlaK)

The two heavy batteries were each equipped with four 8.8cm FlaK18, 36 or 37 anti-aircraft guns while the two light batteries fielded 2cm FlaK30 or 38 and 3.7cm FlaK36, 37 or 43 automatic guns. Besides air-defense, the legendary "88" was used as an anti-tank gun. While it could knock out any tank at medium ranges, could fire rapidly and was extremely accurate, it was less than an ideal anti-tank weapon. It was a large and heavy piece, with a high profile, which made it difficult to conceal. Since these types of weapons needed surprise to be effective, proper concealment was of paramount importance. Emplacing the "88" required a considerable effort on the part of the crew. It was time-consuming to un-limber the "88" to ready it for firing, as well as displace the weapon to alternate positions. The "88" was towed by an expensive and maintenance-intensive halftrack prime mover, usually the mittlerer Zugkraftwagen 8-ton Sd.Kfz.7. The "88" was provided with high explosive and armor-piercing ammunition.

The two light batteries were intended to protect the heavy anti-aircraft guns and the division headquarters from close-in air attack. They were also extensively employed against ground targets. They were especially valuable on the Ostfront in repelling massed infantry attacks, owing to their high rate of fire. The light guns were also useful for suppressing tree lines, defended buildings, and light field fortifications as well as lightly armored vehicles and soft-skin vehicles. The 2cm and 3.7cm FlaK were often mounted on halftracks allowing them to keep pace with the mobile units they supported, while others were towed by light trucks or the Sd.Kfz.10 or Sd.Kfz.11 halftrack prime movers. The 2cm FlaK was provided with high explosive-tracer, armor-piercing-tracer, and improved armor-piercing-tracer rounds. The 3.7cm gun could also fire high explosive, high explosive-tracer, and armor-piercing-tracer rounds.

Uniforms and Insignia

Initially when the division was organized, the troops reported for duty wearing uniforms as diversified as the sources they came from, such as: police dark blue, police green, Heer field gray, old SS earth gray (light brown), and sometimes Czechoslovak olive drab. They were soon issued Heer field gray uniforms, but many of the former Ordnungspolizei officers and NCOs retained their green uniforms for a time, modifying them and attaching the appropriate insignia. The division's men initially wore several distinctive Ordnungspolizei insignia plus other insignia that identified them as members of the Polizei-Division. This applied to all personnel, not just the former Ordnungspolizei.

This variety was most noticeable on the troop's headgear. On field caps the police-type short-winged eagle and swastika in an oval wreath was seen. On the officer's caps the insignia was on a five-sided black backing, while enlisted-men's appeared on a four-sided dark-green backing. On the right side of the steel helmet, the shield-shaped, silver-on-black Ordnungspolizei decal (Waffenschilde) was applied, while the red, white and black swastika decal appeared on the left side.

Light-green, a color historically associated with the German police, was incorporated into the uniform, and was often called "police green". Polizei-Division general officers wore light green greatcoat collars and lapels rather than the Waffen-SS light gray or the Heer bright red. This applied to their trousers' double-stripes as well. One of the division's most notable distinctions was the double bars on the collars of the tunic. They were silver-colored Ordnungspolizei bars on a light green backing rather than the Heer dark blue-green. Officers and enlisted men did wear the dark blue-green collar-facings on tunics and greatcoats. Initially, officers and enlisted men wore light green Waffenfarbe on their shoulder boards/straps regardless of branch.

In 1942, when the division was assigned to the Waffen-SS, the double collar bars were replaced by the silver-colored double SS runes on a black backing along with Waffen-SS collar rank insignia on black backings. Prior to this, SS members wore SS runes on a "police green" backing below their left breast pocket, but it was removed when the collar runes were authorized. At the same time, a silver-edged black cuff band with the police eagle and wreath on it was authorized for wear on the left arm. It was replaced in December by a cuff band inscribed "SS-Polizei-Division" in silver-colored embroidery. It was available in both Gothic and Latin block letter styles. Enlisted men used Waffen-SS black shoulder straps rather than the Heer dark blue-green previously worn. From the division's beginning, the Waffen-SS silver-colored spread-winged eagle and swastika on a black backing was worn centered on the upper left sleeve rather then the Heer-style eagle seen over the right breast pocket. Instead of the white Waffenfarbe worn by infantry units, the Polizei-Division regiments wore light green whether designated as Schützen, Infanterie, Grenadier, or Panzergrenadier. The division staff and replacement units also wore light green Waffenfarbe.

With personnel assigned from the Ordnungspolizei, Heer, and Waffen-SS, it was necessary for an official rank conversion table to be established for NCOs and junior officers, as seen below. There were no enlisted grades in the Ordnungspolizei equivalent to the Heer or SS ranks of "Schütze" and "Oberschütze". It must also be noted that in the artillery (as well as the cavalry, signals, and transport troops) that sergeants (Feldwebel) were traditionally addressed as "Wachtmeister".

Heer	**Waffen-SS**	**Ordnungspolizei**
Gefreiter	SS-Sturmmann	Wachtmeister (less than 2 years)
Obergefreiter	SS-Rottenführer	Wachtmeister (2-4 years)
Unteroffizier	SS-Unterscharführer	Wachtmeister (over 4 years)
Unterfeldwebel	SS-Scharführer	Oberwachtmeister
Feldwebel	SS-Oberscharführer	Revier-Oberwachtmeister
Oberfeldwebel	SS-Hauptscharführer	Hauptwachtmeister
Leutnant	SS-Untersturmfürer	Meister und Obermeister
Oberleutnant	SS-Obersturmführer	Inspektor

Polizei-Artillerie-Regiment troops pose at their barracks. While they wear the Waffen-SS eagle on their sleeves, they wear no decals on their helmets at this time. Note the immaculate appearance of their 10.5cm le.FH18, seen during what is probably a ceremonial occasion.

A 10.5cm le.FH18 howitzer readied for inspection. Note the ropes fastened to the front of the gun shield. Earlier guns had larger shields, but the le.FH18 shield was small in an effort to reduce the gun's weight. The "Kanonier" (gunner) to the right wears the white denim work tunic with field gray trousers.

Two 10.5cm le.FH18 howitzers sit on a Kaserne's parade grounds prior to a maneuver; the troops wear red maneuver bands on their helmets—the opposing side wore yellow bands. The position of the guns and stacked carbines may indicate that new recruits are to be sworn in. It was standard practice for a unit's principal weapons to be present when recruits took the oath of allegiance on the unit standard. An infantry regiment, for example, would display heavy machine guns, mortars, and carbines; a panzer regiment would display its tanks.

The crew of a 10.5cm howitzer poses for the camera. The Waffen-SS eagle can barely be seen on the left sleeve of the man straddling the gun tube. In the foreground, the man to the left is an NCO candidate identifiable by the braid loop at the base of his shoulder straps.

A 10.5cm le.FH18 howitzer stands before the barracks with the divisional band. The bandsmen are identifiable by the "swallows' nests" on both of their shoulders. A bandsman in the center holds the "Jingling Johnny" (Schellenbaum). Regulations allowed these to be individualized by units with distinctive ornamentation. Note the paper tape applied to the barracks's windows as a war-time measure against flying glass.

A 10.5cm le.FH18 battery located on a muddy farm field prepares to fire on a rainy day. Their rifles are stacked to keep them out of the mud. This series of photographs appears to be taken during a training exercise.

Another howitzer from the same battery as in the previous photograph is ready for firing and rapid re-loading. The rate of fire was four-to-six rounds-per-minute. The rain-saturated ground has caused problems though, with the right wheel sinking into it; obviously this affects the gun's accuracy.

Here ammunition is unloaded and placed in small ammunition pits dug near the gun. Once unloaded, the caisson will be moved well to the rear and concealed. The crew has begun throwing up a parapet in front of the gun and digging slit trenches for themselves. The wheels of guns positioned in the open were often covered with tarps or shelter-quarters to aid in concealment. From a distance the exposed wheels stood out.

The photograph is blurred by the concussion of the gun firing as the lanyard is pulled. The Waffen-SS-pattern shelter-quarter covering the wheel is apparent. The gun tube of a 10.5cm le.FH18 had a life of 10,000 to 12,000 rounds before it had to be replaced.

A 3.Batterie gun fires. Hanging beneath the cradle is the muzzle cap secured to the gun by a long leather strap. The crew's rifles are laid on a folded shelter-quarter. In total, the 10.5cm howitzer had a nine-man crew. Usually fewer are seen serving the piece because the three "Fahrers" (drivers) were to the rear with the horses, limber, and caisson.

Ammunition is unloaded from a 10.5cm howitzer's caisson in a harvested field. The low piles are cornstalks and husks. The "Rasputitza" (big mud), caused by the autumn rains beginning in mid-September, have completely saturated the ground.

Ammunition handlers prepare 10.5cm cartridges for firing. They are packed three per wooden box. The white items stacked on a folded shelter-quarter are propellant charge bags, they were removed from cartridges (each was issued containing eight charges), which will be later disposed of.

A gun crew stands by for a fire mission. They would be told the deflection (horizontal angle of fire), elevation (vertical angle of fire), the number of propellant charges, and the type of ammunition to use before loading the gun. The covered aluminum bucket is for unused propellant charges. Aluminum was used rather than steel to prevent a spark from igniting the sensitive charges.

Like so many other soldiers, artillerymen spent a great deal of time waiting; their other three most common activities were: displacing to firing positions, cleaning the gun and its associated equipment, and caring for the horses. Note the open doors of the caisson; the cartridge cases are stowed in the upper portion and the projectiles in the lower.

Crewmen fuse practice projectiles. These weighed the same as high explosive projectiles, but contained only a small marking charge. The projectiles are marked with weight zone markings and "UbB" in white meaning a practice round with a TNT marking charge. The man in the middle holds a fuse wrench, whose leather case is attached to his belt. As it was essential that the projectiles be kept clean, they are laid out on cloth, rather than on the ground.

A view of the ready ammunition station behind the gun. Here the propellant cartridges were issued in metal-lined wicker containers rather than wooden boxes. The Geschützführer to the left looks to the rear at two figures in the distance, that are relaying firing orders. Though blurred, to the left of the gun tube, near the wheel, can be seen an M32 panoramic telescope, the standard sight used on many German artillery pieces.

As one crewman prepares to load a projectile, to the right another waits with a rammer to set the projectile into the chamber, to be followed by a cartridge case. A report/map case and binocular container rest on the near trail. The "Geschützführer" (gun leader), an Unteroffizier, stands to the left. Besides relaying the firing commands, supervising the crew, overseeing the maintenance of the gun and equipment, and the care of the horses, he was also responsible for all safety measures.

The gun crew is visited by the battery's reporting NCO or "der Spiess", here a Wachtmeister. He is armed with a small-caliber pistol and carries binoculars and a report/map case.

The crew of a 10.5cm howitzer stand by awaiting an order to begin a fire mission. Ready ammunition is stacked to the right rear. Normally "Munitionslöcher" (ammunition pits) would be dug for the ammunition, but the saturated ground, and the fact that this is a training scenario, prevents this.

A howitzer crew prepares to load up and move out. Here they disassemble the red- and white-striped aiming stake. Aiming stakes were set up some distance forward of the gun to serve as a reference point from which to set the gun's deflection.

Crewmen riding on the caisson and limber often had to follow on foot to reduce the load's weight in mud, snow, or on rough ground. They might also have to assist by pushing as one crew in the background is doing.

An important piece of battery equipment was the "Feldküche" (field kitchen) with its own limber carrying utensils and cooking gear. The troops referred to it as the "Gulaschkanone" (goulosh cannon) or "Futterkanone" (fodder cannon). Leather tack used for draft horses and enlisted men's horses' equipment was normally dark brown in color. Officer's horse tack was reddish-brown.

Artillery batteries were provided with two 7.92mm MG34 light machine-guns for self-defense, both from ground and air attack. Here an MG34 is mounted on a Dreifuß 34 anti-aircraft tripod, camouflaged with a shelter-quarter and tree limbs. An anti-aircraft ring sight has been fitted.

An MG34 machine-gun set up on an anti-aircraft tripod. The assistant gunner stands by with an M41 machine-gun ammunition box, which held either five 50-round belts (250 rounds, total) or a single 300-round belt. The first photo very clearly shows the shoulder-sleeve insignia, including the Waffen-SS eagle.

While a blurred photograph, this is a rare view of an entire light artillery Abteilung lined up taken during a training exercise. In the foreground is a caisson attached to a limber, while the guns are 7.5cm FK16 n.A (new model) pieces. The white symbol on the sides of the limbers and caissons is that of an artillery unit, which was also used as a tactical map symbol to identify the location of an artillery unit.

Another view of the same unit's light artillery limbers and caissons. Besides serving as limbers for artillery pieces they also towed ammunition caissons. The white artillery unit tactical symbol on the caisson's sides normally had the battery number (1 to 9) beneath it.

A 3.Batterie 7.5cm FK16 n.A (new model) with its limber. Note the seats on the gun shield. These obsolete guns initially equipped Artillerie-Regiment 300 (soon to be re-designated Polizei-Artillerie-Regiment), during training and when it first entered combat.

A 10.5cm le.FH18 howitzer battery halts while passing through a town at night. The details of the folding trail spades are shown here, as are the spade, projectile rammer, and the red- and white-striped aiming stake fastened to the trails. Note the Ordnungspolizei insignia on the side of the helmet at left. The four-point silver-colored star on a dark green-backed insignia on two of the soldiers' greatcoat sleeves is that of "Oberkanonier" (senior cannoneer).

A soldier stands guard beside a group of parked wagons belonging to an artillery battery. These carried baggage, rations, supplies, and equipment. Note that they are parked beneath the trees to better conceal them from observation.

During a training march, the troops wear their white denim work tunics with field gray trousers. These three "Fahrer" (drivers) ride the left-hand-side horses of a six-horse gun team.

Two 10.5cm howitzer crewmen stand by to hitch the gun to its limber as other crewmen ready it for transport. Their gas mask cases are slung to the front to allow them to sit comfortably in the limber's seats.

A battery was assigned two Maschinengewehrschützen (machine-gunners) to man the two 7.92mm MG34s, for self-protection. Other battery personnel would be detailed to assist them when necessary. The gunner wears a white denim work uniform; on the left front of his belt is the leather machine-gun tool case.

A gun crew rests during a halt. Standing behind them is the battery Hauptwachtmeisterdiensttuer (chief sergeant), the reporting NCO or "der Spiess", equivalent to a US Army battery first sergeant or British/Commonwealth battery sergeant major. While officially titled a Hauptwachtmeisterdiensttuer, he could hold the rank of Unteroffizier to Oberwachtmeister; here a Wachtmeister. He is identifiable by the two bands of silver-colored braid on his tunic cuffs. These were known to soldiers as "Kolbenringe" (piston rings).

Battery personnel are assembled to manhandle a 10.5cm howitzer out of a stream, where a hastily-constructed timber bridge has collapsed. The six horses were unable to pull the gun, which weighed 5,589-pounds in travel order, out of the steep-banked stream. Note the pick fastened to the gun shield.

D-rings were fitted to the wheel hubs and their purpose is demonstrated here. The silver-on-black Waffen-SS eagle can be seen on the left sleeves of the men in this photograph.

Manpower does the job.

Earth and logs have been thrown into the stream to make a crude ramp, while the rest of the battery passes over.

A boisterous group of soldiers returns from leave aboard a commandeered farm wagon. The Germans also commandeered any and all horses, civilian and military, to replace their own extensive losses.

Battery NCOs rest against a fence during a halt in their road march. Their ranks are, from left to right, Unteroffizier (corporal), Unterwachtmeister (sergeant), and Wachtmeister (senior sergeant). Besides their leather report/map case (Meldekartentasche), the Wachtmeister wears a field pocket lamp (Feldtaschen Lampe). In the foreground can be seen the pre-war three-tone camouflage pattern used on equipment tarps and tents. The rifle slung on the soldier's back is a 7.92mm Gew98, an earlier version of the slightly shorter Kar98k carbine issued to most units. The Gew98 was issued to many second-line units such as the Polizei-Division.

A light artillery battery wagon and it's team of six horses. This same horse arrangement towed light howitzers with their limber. An artillery draft horse was referred to as a "Kaltblüter" (cold-blooded)—a slow, gentle, heavy horse used as a draft animal. The Kanoniere wear one 30-round, three-pocket carbine pouch on their belts. Normally only infantrymen and pioneers were issued two pouches.

A Kanonier/Fahrer rests atop a bale of hay fitted into the caisson's passenger seat; note the spurs strapped to his boots. The Ordnungspolizei badge can be seen on his cap. The Kanonier standing between the limber and caisson has the Waffen-SS eagle on his tunic sleeve.

A 10.5cm howitzer battery from SS-Artillerie-Regiment 4 halts on its road to war. Note how some soldiers wear their gas mask cases in the "riding" position, and the unit's disposition to one side of the road so that other traffic may pass.

An artillery Abteilung stretches along a road as far as the eye can see, in a photo that was probably taken after the French Campaign. Note how the entire unit is neatly arrayed along one side of the road, allowing other traffic to pass unhindered.

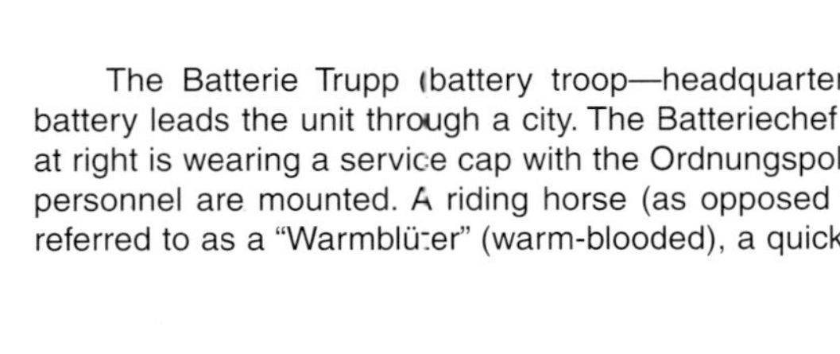

The Batterie Trupp (battery troop—headquarters) of a light artillery battery leads the unit through a city. The Batteriechef (battery commander) at right is wearing a service cap with the Ordnungspolizei badge. All battery personnel are mounted. A riding horse (as opposed to a draft horse) was referred to as a "Warmblüter" (warm-blooded), a quick, agile light horse.

Part of a gun crew walks through a French town. Crewmen would sometimes walk to reduce the load the horses pulled; note the "riding" position of their gas masks. Although there was little likelihood of an Allied gas attack, regulations were strictly enforced and gas masks were carried constantly, even when other equipment was left aboard unit transport. In reality the gas mask case was often used to carry cigarettes, socks, foot wraps, and writing materials leading to the German soldier calling this relatively "weather-proof" item a "Zigarettenbüchse" (cigarette box).

Gun crewmen follow a caisson passing through a French town. Note that these are not young recruits, but older men, who were probably veteran pre-war police officers.

A 10.5cm howitzer is set-up on a French street for emergency employment against tanks. While provided armor-piercing and shaped-charge anti-tank rounds, these guns were far from being effective anti-tank weapons. They were too slow to traverse and elevate and their rate of fire was much too slow.

The lakeside bivouac of a 10.5cm howitzer unit. This photograph demonstrates the number of support wagons and other equipment employed by an artillery Abteilung. Many of the troops are wearing swimming trunks and no doubt the horses have enjoyed the lake as well.

A four-man tent fabricated by buttoning together four Waffen-SS-pattern Zeltbahn shelter-quarters. Designs also existed for eight- and 16-man tents. Besides blankets, soldiers relied on their wool greatcoats for warmth. Straw has been spread on the tent's floor to provide insulation from the cold ground. Note the pair of slippers in the tent's entrance. Civilian slippers were commonly worn when bivouacked. Bread and water was often all that was available for breakfast, although every effort was made to provide coffee, or rather "Ersatz-Kaffee" (substitute coffee).

An artillery Abteilung struggles on its way down a muddy Russian road. Above the gun and to the right of the horses, is a group of men attempting to extract a mired motorcycle combination.

A wide-gauge railroad loading platform. These were built level with flatcars so that when they pulled in, there was a small gap between them and the platform, allowing loads to be entrained or detrained quickly and easily. The ever-present sacks of horse fodder and bales of hay can be seen stacked beside the platform.

Howitzers and caissons await the arrival of a narrow-gauge train on a timber loading platform.

A towing engine switches on to a narrow-gauge mainline. Another sideline switch can be seen ahead. Note the plank corduroy road servicing the rail line; some of these forest facilities could be quite elaborate. A Heer-pattern shelter-quarter tent has been erected on a flatcar.

The Germans made extensive use of narrow-gauge railroads. They could carry surprisingly heavy loads and the flatcars were much wider in proportion to the track than wider gauge rolling stock. Part of this load consists of crates of bottled apple juice, vitally important as its vitamin-C content prevented scurvy; fresh fruit was unheard of on the Ostfront. The narrow-gauge track was provided in pre-fabricated sections and could be laid very quickly. To support the weight on marshy ground so often encountered in Russian forests, a roadbed was first laid of saplings running parallel with the track. This was overlaid with perpendicular logs at less than one-yard intervals, then two lines of squared timbers are laid end-to-end the same width as the track. The track sections were then laid atop the timbers and secured by spikes.

A 10.5cm howitzer battery is loaded aboard a 60cm (23.6-inch) narrow-gauge railroad. The small flatcars allow only a single artillery piece or a single limber to be loaded on each. The little "Schleppe" (towing engine) is nicknamed "Flitzkopp," painted in white. This is a German slang term for an impetuous person, meaning one who dashes ahead without thinking.

This gun crew wears mosquito-proof head nets. Mosquitoes were a major problem in the Russian spring, summer, and fall. The large cloth sacks behind the howitzer carry horse fodder. Note the commandeered chair on the end of the flatcar, to the right.

On the right is a field kitchen, which could simultaneously cook 29-gallons of soup or stew, as well as brew 16-gallons of coffee. Four insulated 12.5-quart food containers were provided to carry the food to gun positions. To fuel the cook fires, the unit could burn coal, coke, charcoal briquettes, or wood. To the left is a captured Soviet mobile cooking cauldron.

An SS-Hauptsturmführer (equivalent to a Heer Hauptmann—captain) on the left, possibly a Batterieführer, and another officer, take a stroll. His Waffen-SS collar rank tab is too blurred to be accurately identified, but he might be an SS-Obersturmführer (equivalent to a Heer Oberleutnant—1st Lieutnant). The Polizei-Division silver-on-black cuff band can be seen on the SS-Hauptsturmführer's left sleeve.

This hastily-established command post was made using a cart camouflaged by straw. A leather map board is carried on this soldier's back, while a leather map tube is seen to the right. The Germans were not issued sleeping bags, but rather a number of wool blankets, here carried in a bedroll.

The crew of a 10.5cm light howitzer poses during a rest break. Ordnungspolizei insignia can faintly be seen on their caps, but they wear no Waffen-SS sleeve insignia on their greatcoats. At least three of the men wear Gefreiter rank insignia consisting of a single chevron.

A meal is quickly consumed during a brief halt from the march. "Feldküchengerichte" (field kitchen dishes) were Spartan consisting mainly of soups and stews. The German soldier's nicknames for such fare was quite creative, often descriptive and usually humorous. For instance, there was "Drahtverhau" (barbed wire entanglement—mixed dried vegetables), "Eintopf" (cabbage soup), "Frontkameradensuppe" (front comrades' soup—a stew of beans, potatoes, and ham—"the comrades"), "Horst Wessel-Suppe" (Horst Wessel soup—a meatless, flavorless soup), and "Wassersuppe" (water soup—a soup with so few ingredients that it was little more than flavored hot water).

This hastily-built shelter was constructed from a destroyed barn. Like the previously-depicted log-framed shelter, it protected the gun, ammunition, and crew from the weather. Note the second shelter to the left on the skyline.

A winter bivouac in Mother Russia, whose soldiers proudly display their phonograph. Such amenities were highly prized possessions.

These men, probably readying for a local security patrol, have been issued the effective Waffen-SS insulated winter coat and mittens, but not the matching trousers or insulated boots. Artillery units were expected to provide their own local security and defense; infantry units were normally not detailed to protect them.

This whitewashed 10.5cm howitzer is further camouflaged with dirty white tarps and fir saplings. The crewmen are cleaning the breechblock, which has been removed, and the firing pin.

Kanonier, Polizei-Division, Panzergruppe 4, Luga, North Russia, August 1941

This figure shows the early war uniform worn by the Polizei-Division from 1939 to early 1942, before it became a part of the Waffen-SS. The Polizei-Division was predominantly formed from members of the Order Police (Ordnungspolizei—Orpo) the uniformed 'civilian' police. Other specialised units were contributed from the Army and the Waffen-SS. It was for the most part uniformed and equipped by the Army and came under SS administrative control. This cooperation of armed forces was reflected in its unique divisional uniform and insignia, incorporating a mixture of Army, Polizei and SS items.

This artilleryman's M35 steel helmet has Polizei decals; the Orpo decal is seen here, the other is the swastika decal on the right side. Tucked into his belt is the M34 Army field cap with standard Polizei emblem insignia. The field cap would be worn when the 'Soldat' was not in action.

The Army M36 field blouse is worn with its distinctive insignia; the Polizei Litzen with their light green (also known as 'police green') backing are sewn on to the dark-green collar. Coming under the administration of the SS meant that the SS eagle and swastika national emblem is worn on his left arm. The shoulder straps are the Army dark-green type usually piped in Polizei/light green. However as this 'Soldat' belongs to the artillery, the branch color was bright red. The service trousers are the M40 field-grey type tucked into his marching boots, although mounted troops of the horse-drawn artillery regiment wore cavalry breeches and riding boots with spurs.

The artilleryman's equipment was basic; the SS enlisted man's leather belt, a rifle ammunition pouch (only one was issued), the M1938 gasmask in its metal canister (with the canister strap worn over the right shoulder for artillerymen), M1931 field flask, S84/98 bayonet, M1931 bread bag and the Army M31 (Zeltbahn) splinter camouflage shelter quarter. Other equipment items were carried on horse-drawn transport. For personal defence he was issued with the Czech vz.24 rifle, which was standard to this division. Small arms such as pistols, rifles and machine guns were supplied from Ordnungspolizei and SS arsenals (which was mainly Czechoslovakian stock). He is holding a Loading Staff (Ladestock) for a 15cm s.FH18 heavy field howitzer.

Leutnant, Polizei-Division, 18.Armee, Leningrad Front, North Russia, October 1941

This Artillery junior officer wears a similar uniform to figure 1 but with the obvious officer characteristics. His headgear is the distinctive Polizei officer's peak cap, with light green piping, dark brown headband and metal Polizei emblem and metal cockade. Alternatively he could wear an Army M38 officer's field cap (the Waffen-SS officer's model field cap was also worn, but not to the same extent as the army type). These field caps would have Polizei emblem insignia and aluminium piping around the crown. Some officers put a metal cockade on their field caps (similar to their peak caps) but this practice was later forbidden.

The uniform consists of an enlisted man's Army M36 field blouse (commonly worn by officers in the field). Sometimes officers would have their blouses altered to give them a more officer-like appearance, but in the case of the Polizei-Division this did not seen to happen that often. On his field blouse the insignia is; the officer's quality Polizei Litzen (hand embroidered in aluminium wire and on a light green backing), Army officer rank shoulder straps (piped in bright red for artillery) and the officer's quality SS sleeve eagle (machine woven in an aluminium thread). The badge on his left breast pocket is the German national sports badge. Also worn in standard officer dress are the officers' riding breeches (in this case with leather reinforcement) and officer's riding boots. Furthermore his boots have spurs due to him being part of an artillery-mounted unit.

Before this division became part of the Waffen-SS, officers and enlisted men used Army rank titles and Army shoulder straps as opposed to using Ordnungspolizei or SS rank titles and shoulder straps.

This Artillery officer's equipment consists of; the SS pattern officer's leather belt (also used was the Army officer's belt with its more secure double claw buckle), 10x50 field binoculars and carrying case (slung over his left shoulder), M35 report/map case. His personal weapon (in its holster) comes from Polizei stock, the very popular Sauer Model 38(h) pistol, one of the most accurate pistols of the period.

SS-Rottenführer, SS-Polizei-Division, 18.Armee, Wolchow Pocket, North Russia, May 1942

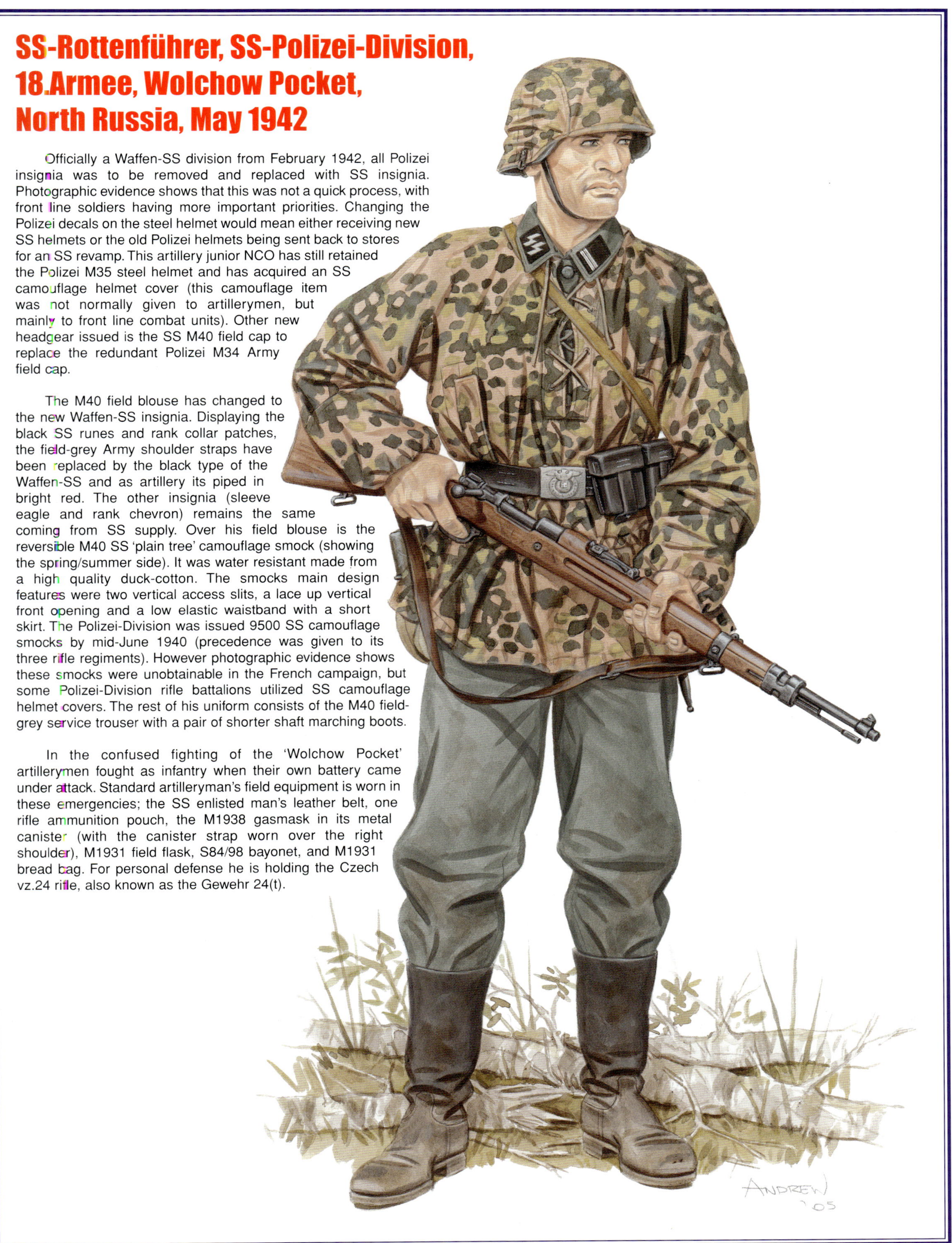

Officially a Waffen-SS division from February 1942, all Polizei insignia was to be removed and replaced with SS insignia. Photographic evidence shows that this was not a quick process, with front line soldiers having more important priorities. Changing the Polizei decals on the steel helmet would mean either receiving new SS helmets or the old Polizei helmets being sent back to stores for an SS revamp. This artillery junior NCO has still retained the Polizei M35 steel helmet and has acquired an SS camouflage helmet cover (this camouflage item was not normally given to artillerymen, but mainly to front line combat units). Other new headgear issued is the SS M40 field cap to replace the redundant Polizei M34 Army field cap.

The M40 field blouse has changed to the new Waffen-SS insignia. Displaying the black SS runes and rank collar patches, the field-grey Army shoulder straps have been replaced by the black type of the Waffen-SS and as artillery its piped in bright red. The other insignia (sleeve eagle and rank chevron) remains the same coming from SS supply. Over his field blouse is the reversible M40 SS 'plain tree' camouflage smock (showing the spring/summer side). It was water resistant made from a high quality duck-cotton. The smocks main design features were two vertical access slits, a lace up vertical front opening and a low elastic waistband with a short skirt. The Polizei-Division was issued 9500 SS camouflage smocks by mid-June 1940 (precedence was given to its three rifle regiments). However photographic evidence shows these smocks were unobtainable in the French campaign, but some Polizei-Division rifle battalions utilized SS camouflage helmet covers. The rest of his uniform consists of the M40 field-grey service trouser with a pair of shorter shaft marching boots.

In the confused fighting of the 'Wolchow Pocket' artillerymen fought as infantry when their own battery came under attack. Standard artilleryman's field equipment is worn in these emergencies; the SS enlisted man's leather belt, one rifle ammunition pouch, the M1938 gasmask in its metal canister (with the canister strap worn over the right shoulder), M1931 field flask, S84/98 bayonet, and M1931 bread bag. For personal defense he is holding the Czech vz.24 rifle, also known as the Gewehr 24(t).

SS-Kanonier, 4.SS-Polizei Panzergrenadier-Division, 11.Armee, Pomerania, Germany, February 1945

In February 1942 new SS winter clothing officially known as 'Special Clothing for Particularly Cold Zones' was issued to the SS-Polizei-Division, during the harsh sub-zero battles on the Leningrad front, in Northern Russia. It consisted of a fur vest, an anorak (that was hooded and fur-lined), a fur cap and fur-lined mittens. A long baggy white cotton hooded smock was also issued for snow camouflage. In the following winter of 1942-43 they received the new model SS fur-lined anorak.

In the final defensive battles of the Third Reich this division's winter uniforms were standard issue like any other Waffen-SS unit, wearing the SS fur-lined anoraks or one of the various SS type greatcoats. Another winter uniform used particularly by this division was the Army field-grey reversible winter suit. Furthermore they were well supplied with this uniform. It was issued to the 'Kampfgruppe SS-Polizei' for the winter of 1943-44. These Army winter uniforms were worn simultaneously with the SS fur-lined anorak, right up to the war's end by this Waffen-SS division.

This SS artilleryman wears the Army winter uniform; it consisted of hooded jacket, trousers and mittens. The material used for the uniform was a padded insulating material with a water-repellent fabric outer shell. The uniform was reversible, a white side for snow camouflage and a grey side for other conditions. He is wearing this reversible winter suit with the grey side outermost. The jacket is open slightly exposing a part of the reversible white side. Under the padded jacket is the SS M43 field blouse with standard Waffen-SS insignia; black SS collar patches, artillery black shoulder straps, SS sleeve eagle and 'SS-Polizei-Division' cuffband (introduced in December 1942). Under the padded winter suit trousers he wears the SS M43 'Keilhose' trousers. He is also wearing an early type SS fur cap. As part of his winter kit he wears the felt and leather winter boots.

This SS-Kanonier holds a 10.5cm shell and is wearing the minimum of equipment; the SS enlisted man's leather belt, a P38 pistol in its 'soft-shell' holster, slung over the holster is an SS M42 steel helmet crudely painted in whitewash for snow camouflage.

Another crew poses beside their 10.5cm howitzer in a winter setting. No effort has been made to prepare a position or even seriously camouflage it other than laying a tarp atop the gun. They will probably only occupy the position for a short time.

This whitewashed 10.5cm howitzer is further camouflaged with white sheets. The sheet flapping in the breeze beneath the barrel could call attention to the position, since any moving object will catch the eye of an observer. The hood-like caps were issued with the winter insulated suits and designed to be worn beneath the steel helmet.

This 10.5cm le.FH18/40 howitzer combined the 10.5cm gun and cradle with a PaK40 carriage, wheels and trails, along with a newly-designed shield. At 4,310-pounds (travel and firing order), it was lighter than the standard le.FH18 (seen in the background), which weighed 5,589-pounds in travel order and 4,377-pounds in firing order. The le.FH18/40 was normally equipped with a muzzle break (not seen fitted here; note the bare metal and threads at the muzzle end of the gun tube), which would have been an essential piece of equipment when firing the gun since the carriage was much lighter than the standard piece. The standard howitzer in the background has cast steel wheels. The visiting officer is an SS-Obersturmführer.

The same 10.5cm howitzer battery, in position as seen from the rear. Batteries typically repositioned themselves several times a day to keep pace with the advancing infantry and to avoid being targeted by enemy artillery.

Two officers, an SS-Hauptsturmführer to the left and an SS-Untersturmführer to the right, pose in front of their troops. The SS-Untersturmführer wears the Iron Cross 1st Class and a Wound Badge on his left breast pocket.

The battery moves out to the next firing position. Normally when the unit was engaged, each battery within an Abteilung relocated at different times so that one or two were always in position ready to provide immediate fire support.

A gun crew poses before their hastily prepared dugout (Unterschlupfe), or what solders called a dwelling bunker (Wohnbunker). Any and all materials were used to construct such shelters; artillery projectile packing fames have been used here. In the background is a large staff tent probably sheltering the Batterie - Trupp (battery headquarters).

In the Russian winter, sleds were much better suited for hauling supplies and equipment, than wagons. The Germans adopted the Russian word for sled, "Pulk". They were typically drawn by one or two hardy Russian ponies.

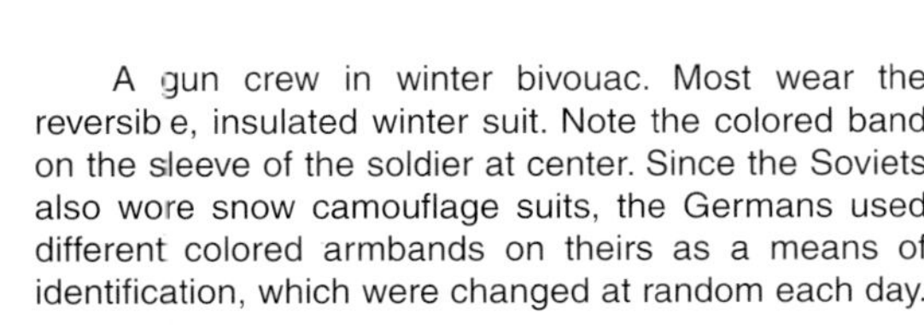

A gun crew in winter bivouac. Most wear the reversible, insulated winter suit. Note the colored band on the sleeve of the soldier at center. Since the Soviets also wore snow camouflage suits, the Germans used different colored armbands on theirs as a means of identification, which were changed at random each day.

Artillerymen watch with concern as a caisson is pulled over a makeshift bridge. The iron-rimmed wheels could easily slip off in such icy conditions. The hood of the Waffen-SS-issue fur-lined winter jacket is seen on one of the men near the center.

This 10.5cm le.FH16 howitzer is positioned in a log-frame shelter covered by thick layers of fir boughs. Such a shelter offered no real protection from artillery fire but protected the gun, ammunition, and crew from the brutal weather as well as providing a degree of concealment.

A 10.5cm le.FH16 howitzer in an open position camouflaged with fir saplings.

A 10.5cm howitzer position in a snow-covered field. Besides the white smoke generated when firing, the muzzle blast would raise a great deal of snow powder that would drift slowly to the ground, making it easy for enemy observers to detect the firing position.

The crew of a well-camouflaged piece (its gun tube can be seen to the left), pose in front of their position. While the piece is almost completely concealed, the position actually takes on a "piled-on" appearance, which can stand out to observers. The crew wears mostly standard tunics, but various other winter uniform components can be seen.

Despite the power of six horses, this crew has to provide an assist as the team strains to drag this gun and limber up a gradual slope. Iron-shod horse hooves had difficulty gaining a purchase on icy snow. This is a 10.5cm le.FH16 light field howitzer, a World War I weapon adopted in 1916. It was widely used before the war, but relegated to second-line units when the more modern 10.5cm le.FH18 was fielded.

A 10.5cm le.FH16 light field howitzer in a firing position with saplings and brush stacked for concealment. Two seats for crewmen were fitted on the front of the shield either side of the gun tube, on which they rode during travel. Projectiles and their packing tubes are seen beside the gun. The le.FH16 had a feeble range of 1,203 yards as opposed to the le.FH18's 11,678 yards.

This 10.5cm le.FH18 has just ejected a spent cartridge. The wheel, as found on most German artillery pieces, consisted of a heavy duty cast steel hub with a solid rubber rim. This type of tire allowed relatively high-speed towing by a motorized vehicle. Unlike inflatable tires, they had the advantage of being immune to blowouts and light shell fragmentation damage. The hard rubber rim would wear down, but could be replaced. Note the spade and handspike fastened to the gun's trails, as well as the foundry casting symbols on the wheel hub.

This photo depicts a battery of 10.5cm le.FH18s in firing position. Normally there were four guns in a battery, but as losses mounted surviving guns were sometimes consolidated into larger batteries. Possibly parts of two batteries can be seen here; note the dispersal of the guns in a "staggered row" formation and the distance the ammunition is stacked to the rear. The guns appear to be positioned about 30 yards apart.

Two 10.5cm howitzer crewmen clean their gun's limber. The gun's trails were fastened to the limber, which, in turn, was hitched to a team of horses. The limber itself carried gun equipment, accessories, spare parts, and hand tools. Note the camouflage pattern which indicates the limber is finished in the early war two-tone scheme of Dunkelgrau Nr.46 and Dunkelbraun Nr.45.

This 10.5cm le.FH18 leichte Feld Haubitze (light field howitzer) has been demolished by Soviet counter-battery fire, with the shield and right wheel being destroyed. Note that the horizontal sliding breech block is in the open position. The gun was positioned among fir saplings and further camouflaged by cut saplings stacked around it.

A 15cm s.FH18 schwere Feld Haubitze (heavy field howitzer) sits beneath a hastily erected camouflage net. The bare net, unadorned by vegetation or garnishing, provided little concealment. Besides concealing the weapon, camouflage nets also served to deny the enemy the ability to identify what type of artillery piece occupied the position or if the position was actually occupied by a real gun.

Sd.Kfz. 7 halftracks towing 10cm guns prepare to move out. This appears to be a training scene owing to the neatness of the uniforms and lack of additional equipment. There are also rifle targets lined up on the ridge in the background. This photograph s very likely from the pre-war period since the halftracks are in the three-tone "Buntfarbenanstrich" camouflage scheme of Nr.17 Erdgelb, Nr.18 Braun and Nr.28 Grün, plus they lack the Notek black-out driving head-lamp, which was generally not seen in use until after the French Campaign. One of the halftracks is towing an ammunition caisson of the type used by horse-drawn artillery units.

This view of a 10cm s.K18 depicts it in the travel position. The gun tube appears shorter as it has been retracted past the "recoil" position to lessen the overall length of the piece and shift the weight more towards the limber for a better balance of the load. The white "C" on the hydro-pneumatic equilibrator cylinders identifies the gun within the battery. They were designated by the German phonetic letters—Anton, Bertha, Caesar, and Dora—used for transmitting alphabetical letters by radio and telephone so they could be understood through static or a poor connection. The type of cast steel wheel with rubber rims, pictured here, was intended for motorized towing. The prime-mover is an early KMm10 mittlerer Zugkraftwagen 8-ton Sd.Kfz.7; it could also tow the 15cm s.FH, 10cm s.K and 8.8cm FlaK.

The crew of this 10cm (actually 10.5cm) s.K18 schwere Kanone (heavy gun) prepares to load. Note the projectiles, which are painted Feldgrau (a dark grey-green) with white markings. German field artillery ammunition was of the separate-loading-type. The projectile and cartridge case are two separate components; the projectile was loaded first followed by the cartridge. The cartridge case contained eight propellant bags (charges). Charges would be removed from the cartridge depending on the desired range. Ammunition and cartridge boxes can be seen beyond the gun; note the mat beneath the wheel, which prevented the gun from sinking into the soft ground. A level gun was essential to maintain accuracy. The gun is fairly well-concealed by live and cut fir saplings.

A battery of 10cm guns fire a mission at night generating massive muzzle flashes. It was these muzzle flashes that enemy observers searched for when they directed counter-battery fire.

This 10cm gun appears to be located at a maintenance depot, where it lacks the recoil cylinder seen over the gun tube. This view provides an excellent image of the heavy-duty rubber wheel rims. The 10cm gun was mainly intended for long-range counter-battery fire and had a range of 20,870 yards. It was considered too heavy for its intended duties, so efforts were made to develop a lighter, longer-ranged gun for this role, but the 10cm s.K18 remained in use throughout the war. It used the same carriage as the 15cm s.FH18.

The crew of a 15cm s.FH18 "settle-in" the gun. The spades have been dug-in and will be set when the crew fires their adjusting rounds. Fir saplings have been cut and piled around the ground in preparation for camouflaging the gun and its position. The gun is ideally positioned adjacent to a wood line so that when the saplings are laid against the weapon it will blend naturally into the tree-line, rather than looking like a pile of stacked saplings sitting on open ground. The wheels are the cast-aluminum-type with steel rims issued to horse-drawn artillery units.

The business end of a 15cm howitzer cleaned and polished for inspection in a Kaserne (barracks). Note the pre-war camouflage paint, consisting of Dunkelgrau Nr.46 and Dunkelbraun Nr.45. visible on the two elevating cylinders along with the gun's designation, "A"—Anton.

This photo depicts a 15cm howitzer firing, but not yet in full recoil. The gun leader is in his standard position giving the command to fire, which was relayed by the battery commander. The gun-layer, who aims the gun, is seated to the left of the breech. A 15cm howitzer had a 15-man crew.

This 15cm howitzer is in full recoil, while an ammunition handler to the rear stands by with a projectile for the next shot. Beside him are propellant cartridge containers. To the right are wicker projectile containers, which artillerymen called a "Koffer" (suitcase). A four-man tent has been constructed using four Zeltbahn shelter-quarters, with a red- and white-striped aiming stake used as the center pole.

When drawn by horses, the 15cm howitzer was broken down into two loads, each drawn by six horses. Here the carriage and mounting are seen, with equipment secured to the gun's trails. The gun tube and breech was carried on a special four-wheel transport wagon, seen to the right.

Here the gun tube and breech of the 15cm howitzer are seen on its transport wagon traveling through a Russian forest. The transport wagon used the same wheels as the gun carriage. The crewmen are wearing only minimal equipment with the rest being carried aboard limbers, caissons, and the transport wagon. The men on foot carry their gas mask containers in the normal dismounted troops' position while those on horseback wear theirs as specified for mounted soldiers. Although the transport wagon was fitted with seats, crewmen often preferred to walk as the un-sprung wagon was uncomfortable, while the less the horses had to haul, the better for all concerned.

These 15cm howitzers are positioned among fir trees to provide a well-concealed firing position. Saplings and brush have been laid out to be used to further conceal the guns when not firing.

The barrel transport wagon of the 15cm howitzer is backed up to the carriage, where the gun tube and breech will be slid into the mount using a block-and-tackle, which has not yet been rigged. A well-trained crew could accomplish this in a short time. Note the red- and white-striped aiming stakes fastened to the side of the piece's trail.

Another view of a 15cm howitzer carriage with the gun tube removed. The piece's trails are piled high with equipment and accessories.

A 15cm howitzer assembled for firing, probably during training; note the sign next to the tracks. A team of horses could tow the fully assembled piece short distances for positioning. A narrow-gauge railroad, laid by the Germans to haul supplies, parallels the well-maintained road.

A 15cm howitzer in full recoil. The gun could be traversed 64-degrees (32-degrees each side of the center-line). Note how the crewmen plug their ears with their fingers in a vain attempt to preserve their hearing.

The 15cm howitzer's maximum elevation was 45-degrees; it could be depressed 3-degrees.

A 21cm Mrs18 heavy mortar in firing position. This same carriage was used for the 17cm s.K18 gun. In the foreground is what appears to be the burned remains of a Soviet artillery piece.

A complete artillery regiment required some 7,400 yards of road space in a march column, or more than four miles. Note the SS-style camouflage on the rain capes of the troops.

This massive weapon is a 21cm Mrs18 heavy mortar. It was not assigned to divisional artillery, but to army- or corps-level artillery formations, which could be tasked to support a division. It could toss 266.8-pound high explosive or 285.3-pound anti-concrete projectiles up to approximately 18,300 yards. Note the huge limber wheel to the right, partly concealed by saplings.

Riding horses were provided to the part of an artillery crew that did not ride on the limber and caisson. These horsemen wear Waffen-SS camouflage pattern shelter-quarters. The equipment for troop service horses (Ausrüstung des Truppend enstpferdes) included the M25 army saddle, bit and single-snaffle bridle, dark gray saddle blanket, and saddle bags of several types.

The crew of a 10.5cm le.FH16 howitzer poses beside their gun, which is positioned behind a brushwood revetment. The crew wears a mix of uniforms including the standard tunic, greatcoat, and insulated winter suit. Wood-frame carriers for the projectiles can be seen in the lower right. German artillery rounds could be issued in wooden boxes, wood-frame carriers, or wicker containers.

Artillery troops head for Russian houses seeking shelter from a blizzard. Their greatcoats offered little protection from the brutal Russian winter, during which temperatures frequently dropped past 40°F below zero.

The breech-end of a 10.5cm le.FH18 howitzer during transport. The breech and barrel slide are protected by a rubberized canvas cover, as is the optical gun sight (there would also be a similar cover over the muzzle). An elevation/range table is painted on the shield to the left of the gun tube. This particular gun is "D"—Dora. The pair of straps running off frame to the right allows the "Fahrer" (driver) on the limber to set or release the gun's breaks.

Another difficult stream crossing in Russia. Frozen ice and snow often gave way after some traffic had passed over, creating a mass of sticky mud. The log in the foreground will probably be used as a lever to assist in the gun's extraction.

Weather and fatigue took its toll on draft horses just as it did on men. The division's veterinary company was critical for caring for fatigued, sick, injured, and wounded horses and returning them to duty.

A 15cm howitzer fires. Note that on either side are high wooden plank covers with vegetation wired to the outsides, much like a hunter's "blind". When not firing, these were lowered over the piece to conceal it from aerial observation and protect it from snow. The piece's designation within the battery, "C", is marked in white on the recoil cylinder bracket.

The heavy carriage of a 15cm howitzer has slid off the ice-covered road. The steel-rimmed wheels offered no traction on ice or wet hard-surfaced roads. Among the scattered gun equipment are bales of hay for the draft horses. It was essential that fodder be carried for the horses in the winter when no grazing grass was available. Note the crew's helmets fastened to the piece's trail.

A battery of 10.5cm le.FH18 howitzers are lined up to load aboard railroad flat cars during one of the Polizei-Division's many moves. The howitzers are attached to their limbers, with bales of hay on the gun trails for the draft horses. Note the difference in wheel types and the fact that the second howitzer is the "M" version with a muzzle brake. The guns are painted with light-colored stripes over the Dunkelgrau RAL 7021 base color. The evenly spaced paint dabs on the wheel rims actually detract from the camouflage effect since orderly camouflage patterns attract the eye rather than disrupt the appearance of the piece of equipment.

Crews prepare to load their howitzers and limbers on to flatcars. The crews themselves were expected to perform the labor and secure the guns with rope, chains, and wood blocks. When one considers the number of moves any division made, this laborious evolution became routine. Note the piles of debris to the upper right indicating the rail-yard had been heavily bombed at one time, probably by the Germans, who later repaired it for their own use.

A 10.5cm howitzer is manhandled on to a flat car by artillerymen wearing reversible, insulted winter suits (with the mouse-gray side showing, although there is snow on the ground). One gun and limber could be carried on a flat car. The team of six draft horses was carried in a box car.

The workhorse of German divisional artillery was the 10.5cm le.FH18(M). The "(M)" indicated the piece was fitted with a Mündungsbremse (muzzle brake). This was a 1940 modification to achieve longer range by using a heavier propellant charge. Its effective range was 13,483 yards as opposed to the original model's 11,678 yards. When armor-piercing discarding-sabot rounds were later introduced it was found they could not be fired from weapons with muzzle brakes, but a slight modification corrected this deficiency. This piece is fitted with wood-spoke wheels for horse-towing, and has been partly whitewashed to provide an effective camouflage. The crew wears insulated winter uniforms with the Heer-style camouflage-side out. Ready cartridge cases sit nearby for rapid loading.

A 21cm Mrs18 fires a round, the massive concussion jarring the photographer and his camera. The crew wears insulated winter uniforms, camouflage-side out.

The crew of an 8.8cm FlaK36 or 37 relaxes in Russia. Normally the "88" was served by a 10-man crew plus a halftrack driver, who was not considered part of the crew. The Dunkelgrau RAL 7021-colored gun has been over-painted with a lighter color in angular stripes. The weather appears rainy, so the crew's Zeltbahn shelter-quarters have been spread on the ground to dry out. Note the gun accessories partly concealed within the brush. The forest on the horizon appears to be burning from an artillery barrage.

A FlaK18 fires at a ground target. A difficulty encountered with engaging ground targets was the smoke and large amount of dust raised by the considerable muzzle blast. The Kanonenführer (gun leader) stands atop one of the weapon's two Sd.Ah.201 limbers to gain a better view of the target and relay corrections to the Richtkanonier (gun-layer). The "88" could be fired while mounted on its limbers, but the instability affected accuracy and the rate of fire. This was referred to as "Feldmässig". While some of the crewmen have slung their carbines across their shoulders, others have left theirs rather haphazardly lying on the ground. They were usually stacked or laid in an orderly manner. A line of ammunition handlers is passing the heavy rounds to the loader; the projectile alone weighed 21 pounds. White kill rings can be seen painted near the muzzle on the gun tube.

An 8.8cm FlaK18 of SS-Flak-Abteilung 4, assigned to 4.SS-Polizei-Panzergrenadier-Division is positioned for the air-defense role. The gun and its limbers have been lightly camouflaged with cut foliage to help conceal their silhouettes from low flying aircraft. Crews were provided with camouflage nets, but these were time consuming to erect and dismantle, so they were often not used during short halts.

On a hot summer day in Russia, the crew of an 8.8cm gun prepare for a fire mission. Although they are shirtless because of the heat, helmets were still required during action. The gun's position has been camouflaged by placing sunflower plants and clumps of weeds about it, which are wilting. The position is partly dug-in, with the earth held in place by horizontal saplings.

Night firing of the "88" reveals the massive muzzle flash. Lacking a muzzle brake, which reduced the flash somewhat, also made the gun's firing easily detectable when employed in the anti-tank role. The muzzle flash also dazzled the crew and destroyed their night vision making it difficult to acquire targets and rapidly re-aim the gun (although when firing in an anti-aircraft mode, the guns were centrally controlled). The gun's limbers were sometimes positioned nearby, especially if employed in the anti-tank role where it was necessary to rapidly limber-up and re-position the gun. However, the normal practice was to position them out of the crew's way to allow unhampered access to the gun and the nearby ammunition stockpile.

An 8.8cm FlaK36 fires at enemy aircraft. A hastily constructed position of this type was referred to as "Feldmässiger Ausbau", which sited a piece dismounted from the carriage and positioned behind a hasty earth, sand, rock, log, sandbag, or packed snow parapet. These guns had to be centrally-controlled in this mode; note the cable reel on the near limber as well as the cable on the ground to the right in the photo. This veteran piece of ordnance boasts 20 kill rings (Abschußringe) in four groups of five.

A whitewashed 8.8cm FlaK18 has been positioned beside a Russian log cabin. The locals called these an "Isba", with the name being adopted by German soldiers. Note the low tire on the limber in the foreground.

A 2cm FlaK30 crew fires on a Soviet aircraft. The earth parapet is reinforced with planks. This type of position was called a "Verstärkter Feldmässiger Ausbau", which was a deliberately constructed position of planks and timber, brick, or concrete. Such positions usually had a canvas tarp to cover the gun and its equipment. The number of guns assigned to light FlaK batteries varied over time, but was typically twelve 2cm and/or 3.7cm guns in four platoons of three.

A 2cm FlaK30 rattles off rounds during training. Its practical rate of fire was 120 rpm, owing to the 20-round magazines used on German 2cm FlaK pieces. Spare magazines can be seen stacked to the gun's left, while the gun's accessories, including a spare barrel container, are to the right. The FlaK30 was an older model that was being replaced by the FlaK38. However, it remained in use to the war's end.

While not organic to SS-Artillery-Regiment 4, 15cm Nebelwerfer 41 multiple rocket launcher units were sometimes attached to the division. They could fire their high explosive or smoke rockets to over 7,000 yards. It required approximately 90 seconds to re-load the six rockets. The term "Nebelwerfer" means "smoke projector". "Nebel" can also be translated as "fog", but in the military context, it means screening smoke.

The division's infantry regiments possessed their own artillery in the form of four or six 7.5cm le.IG18 leichte Infanteriegeschütze (light infantry guns). These weapons were assigned to the regiment's 13.Kompanie. Note the vegetation attached to the gun's shield. In theory, an infantry regiment's infantry gun company also had two 15cm s.IG33s, but the Polizei-Division did not receive these. Infantry guns were manned by specially-trained infantrymen rather than artillerymen, who were outfitted with complete infantry equipment. The crewmen wear black Waffen-SS runes on a white shield on the right sides of their helmets. These are mostly obscured by a web bread-bag strap commonly used to secure camouflage materials to break up the helmet's silhouette.

The crew of this 7.5cm PaK.40 anti-tank gun wears the reversible (white-side out; mouse gray or camouflage pattern on the inside), insulated, two-piece winter suit. The photographer caught the piece in full recoil as the cartridge case was being ejected. This weapon was sometimes issued to artillery units in lieu of light artillery when nothing more suitable was available.

An anti-tank gun crew in a Russian village readies for firing, while ammunition handlers hold down the gun trails since the spades were not able to dig into the frozen hard-packed ground. This is a 7.5cm PaK97/38, which consisted of a French 75mm mle.1897 gun tube and breech mounted on a German 5cm PaK38 carriage. This was a stop-gap measure to field weapons capable of defeating Soviet T-34 and KV-series tanks. The gun tube was fitted with a perforated, cylindrical Solothurn muzzle brake to mitigate the recoil on the relatively light-weight carriage. Field gray-painted ammunition boxes rest to the rear. The crew wears reversible, insulated winter uniforms, white-side out.

This is a Soviet 85mm M1939 anti-aircraft gun overrun by the Polizei-Division outside of Leningrad. Though obviously prepared to engage aircraft, the Soviets often employed them in the anti-tank role in the same manner the Germans used the "88". The 85mm AA guns was sometime pressed into German service where it was known as the 8.5cm FlaK M39(r). The "(r)" identified a captured piece of equipment as being "russisch", or of Russian-origin. Some were re-bored to use German 8.8cm ammunition. In that case the designation was 8.5/8.8cm FlaK M39(r).

A small number of captured French Schneider 220mm mle.1916 breech-loading mortars were used during the Leningrad siege. The Germans designated it as a 22cm Mrs531(f). The mortar could lob a 221-pound shell 11,000 yards at a rate of two rounds per minute. The meaning of the legend "St." is unknown; it was used for a number of abbreviations in the Wehrmacht, but none apply to a gun designation.

The French Schneider 155mm C mle.1917 howitzer was sometimes issued as a substitute for the 15cm heavy howitzer. The Germans called it the "15.5cm s.FH414(f)". They also used it as a coast defense weapon, not as an anti-ship gun, but to shell the assault troops. It fired a 96.16-pound shell out to 12,362 yards. The howitzer has been positioned on a plank platform behind a two-layer log breastwork.

Another view of a French 155mm C mle.1917, also known as the 15.5cm s.FH414(f). A few saplings have been stuck into the ground as minimal camouflage to include one wired to the "dead-man" post to the right. To this is fastened block-and-tackle by which the gun is pulled back into a protected bunker. The foot ramps on either side provide the loaders with firm footing as they carry the 96.16-pound projectiles to the piece.

It was common for captured artillery pieces to be pressed into German service to make up for losses or augment the guns on hand. Here a Soviet 76.2mm M1927 infantry gun is limbered up. Four horses were required to tow the gun and it's limber. It was typical for more gear to be carried on the limber, including personal baggage and spare clothing wrapped in canvas tarps. The Germans designated this piece as the "7.62cm Infanteriekanonenhaubitze (I.K.H.—infantry cannon howitzer) 290(r). In the center of this photo stands a Stabsgefreiter; the Waffen-SS eagle can be seen over his two rank chevrons. Heer rank insignia and Ordnungspolizei double-collar bars were still being worn at this time. The man to the right carries a collapsible canvas water bucket for the horses.

A similarly camouflaged Soviet 122mm M1938 howitzer has been impressed into German service as the 12.2cm s.FH396(r). This was one of the best and most reliable Soviet artillery pieces of the war, being highly valued by the Germans. It had a range of 12,909 yards. The man to the right is an SS-Rottenführer, identified by the double chevrons and left collar patch. The right collar patch displays the SS runes. The man to the left wears a field gray denim work tunic unadorned with insignia.

This collection of weapons are mostly French-made Schneider 105mm mle.1919 mountain guns formerly used by the Yugoslavians. The Germans employed them as the 10.5cm leichte Gebirgshaubitze (l.Geb.H.—light mountain howitzer) 329(j). It could be broken down into eight pack-horse loads; the gun tube could be disassembled into two parts to ensure that no single load was too heavy. Some of these guns have had whitewash applied for winter camouflage.